Guidance from the Licensing Authority on the Adventure Activities Licensing Regulations 2004

The Activity Centres (Young Persons' Safety) Act 1995

HSE Books

Contents

071337

Foreword

Much of the material in this publication was first issued to accompany the establishment of the adventure activities licensing regime in 1996. The regulations were revised in 2004 and the Health and Safety Executive (HSE) started a revision of the guidance. The announcement by the Chancellor of the Exchequer, in the Budget Statement of 2005, that the government had accepted the recommendation of the Hampton report and that the existing Adventure Activities Licensing Authority (AALA) would merge with HSE meant the revision was postponed until the new regime began to take shape.

HSE was designated as AALA from 1 April 2007 and Tourism Quality Services Ltd (TQS), the private company previously designated as AALA, has been contracted as the Adventure Activities Licensing Service (AALS) to provide most of the administrative and inspection functions on behalf of HSE. Providers will not see much difference on a day-to-day basis but the legal position is different and this second edition of the guidance reflects the new position.

Although much of L77 has stood the test of time and is still relevant today, a number of changes have been made. These:

(a)   reflect the designation of HSE as AALA;
(b)   adopt the lessons learned through the previous years of operation; and
(c)   clarify areas that have been causes of confusion in the past.

The opportunity has also been taken to fully update the technical content where required.

This guidance is from HSE in its role as AALA and is aimed at all those involved in the regime, whether they are:

(a)   exercising AALA functions on behalf of HSE;
(b)   providers of adventure activities; or
(c)   involved in health and safety enforcement.

Providers who do not require a licence, such as schools providing activities to their own pupils, may also find this guidance of use when planning and delivering activities.

Change of licensing authority

HSE was designated AALA with effect from 1 April 2007 but has contracted Tourism Quality Services Ltd (TQS), the not-for-profit company that was previously the AALA, to administer the scheme, carry out inspections and issue licences on HSE's behalf. The contractor is trading as the Adventure Activity Licensing Service (AALS).

In this guidance, references to AALA should be read as meaning HSE and where appropriate, the officers and employees of the contractor.

Outline of the licensing scheme

Aim of the licensing scheme

1   The aim of the adventure activities licensing scheme is to give assurance that good safety management practice is being followed so that young people can continue to have opportunities to experience exciting and stimulating activities outdoors while not being exposed to avoidable risks of death and disabling injury. The requirements on providers are drawn from existing health and safety legislation. The scheme provides assurance that providers have been inspected and have demonstrated compliance with relevant health and safety legislation.

2   Anyone who provides, in return for payment, adventure activities covered by the Regulations to young people under 18 years of age must have a licence and abide by its conditions. The scheme is aimed at those who sell adventure activities to schools and to the public. It does not cover activities offered by voluntary associations to their members, schools to their own pupils or provision for young people accompanied by their parents or legal guardians.

3   The following activities are within scope of the scheme:

(a)   caving (underground exploration in natural caves and mines including potholing, cave diving and mine exploration, but not in those principally used as show-places open to the public);
(b)   climbing (climbing, traversing, abseiling and scrambling activities except on purpose-designed climbing walls or abseiling towers);
(c)   trekking (walking, running, pony trekking, mountain biking, off-piste skiing and related activities when done in moor- or mountain-country above 600 metres and which is remote, ie over 30 minutes travelling time from the nearest road or refuge);
(d)   watersports (canoeing, rafting, sailing and related activities when done on the sea, tidal waters or larger non-placid inland waters).

4   Further guidance on the providers and activities in scope of the licensing scheme is given in Appendix 1.

The licensing authority's role

5   The Regulations set out the legal framework within which the licensing authority must work. The Regulations require the licensing authority:

(a)   to consider **applications** for licences (including renewals and requests for changes); applications must give the authority necessary information and be accompanied by the requisite fee;
(b)   to get a **report** by an authorised person which enables it to decide if the applicant meets the requirements on management of safety;
(c)   to **decide** on the application and, only if it is satisfied, grant a licence. The licence may restrict what the licence-holder can do and must have standard conditions on management of safety and rights for the licensing authority to make further inspections and get further information. The licensing authority can also add non-standard conditions if needed to secure safety in the particular case;
(d)   to **revoke or vary** licences or licence conditions to secure safety. These could arise from a spot-check inspection, investigation of a complaint or in response to a request from the licence-holder;
(e)   to investigate **complaints** which are within its remit and tell the complainant the results and what it has done;
(f)   to make information about licence-holders available to the public.

6   The licensing authority will have regard to this guidance in exercising its statutory functions.

Guiding principles for the licensing authority

7   In exercising its functions, the licensing authority will have regard to the following principles:

(a)   **proportionality**: taking action appropriate to the risks;

(b)   **consistency**: taking a similar approach in similar circumstances to achieve similar ends;

(c)   **targeting**: making sure priorities for inspections focus on where the hazards are least well controlled and where there are the most serious risks;

(d)   **transparency**: making it easy for providers to understand what is expected of them and distinguish between what is advice and what is compulsory; helping the public to identify providers with good safety management practices.

Guidance on safety standards

Framework

8   The primary duty to ensure the safety of young people using facilities for adventure activities rests with the provider of those facilities. The provider must therefore have a systematic approach to recognising risks and making sure that something is done to control them – a safety management system. The licensing scheme is founded on assuring good safety management. This is also the foundation of the Health and Safety at Work etc Act 1974 (the HSW Act) which applies to all the activities offered by most of the providers subject to licensing, whether these activities are in the licensing scheme or outside it.

9   In deciding whether a provider meets the requirements related to safety, the licensing authority will assess whether the provider has a systematic approach to the management of safety, including the implementation, monitoring and review (see also paragraph 18) of the control measures taken to control risks – ie an overall culture of safety.

10   The authority may take account of any relevant evidence that comes to its attention in reaching its decisions, including that from non-licensable activities. If the licensing authority has concerns about the safety of activities outside the Regulations, it will tell the provider and, if those concerns are significant, the relevant enforcing authority. If there is an appropriate National Governing Body (NGB) for the activities concerned, the licensing authority may also bring its concerns to the NGB's attention (see also paragraph 13).

Relevant published guidance

11   The requirements related to safety set out in the Regulations draw on existing health and safety legislation. In considering whether the applicant for a licence has satisfied the requirements related to safety, the licensing authority will have regard to other relevant general guidance issued by the Health and Safety Commission and Executive (see *Further reading*). The licensing authority will also have regard to guidance in the publications of relevant NGBs where that guidance is relevant to the safety of participants at the hazard level of the activity to which the application relates. Where no NGB exists for an activity, the licensing authority will take account of other appropriate guidance and information. For

example, for activities such as sea-level traversing, guidance published by the British Canoe Union (BCU) and Mountain Leader Training UK (MLTUK) may both be relevant.

The risk assessment (regulation 6(1)(a)(i))

12   Before granting a licence, the authority must be satisfied that the provider has:

(a)   identified the hazards created by the activity;
(b)   decided who might be harmed, and how;
(c)   evaluated the risk and decided whether existing measures (safety precautions) are adequate or whether more should be done;
(d)   implemented the measures;
(e)   have arrangements in place for appropriate review and revision of the assessment.

13   As part of their application, providers must set out the significant findings of their risk assessment, the control measures in place and the arrangements relating to it. A provider with more than five employees needs to record these matters to comply with other health and safety legislation. It may be appropriate in many cases, to make reference to relevant NGB guidance for the management of some of the generic risks. This may include any requirements imposed by a NGB under any accreditation or registration scheme.

14   The scope of the risk assessment should be sufficient to identify the significant (non-trivial) risks arising from the activity. It should enable the provider to identify and prioritise the measures that need to be taken to ensure, so far as is reasonably practicable, the safety of participants or others who may be affected by the activity. The licensing authority may include a non-standard condition that restricts the facilities for adventure activities covered by any licence so they are no wider than those set by the provider in the risk assessment.

Measures (regulation 6(1)(a)(ii)) and arrangements (regulations 6(1)(a)(iii) and 9(1)(a))

15   The provider's safety measures should be appropriate to:

(a)   the site(s) and the hazard level at which the activities are to be undertaken;
(b)   the participants' age, experience and any special educational needs.

16   In assessing a provider's safety management system, the licensing authority will look for evidence of the following:

(a)   a policy which creates a culture of safety overall;
(b)   organisational arrangements to turn the policy into practice;
(c)   systematic planning methods;
(d)   appropriate monitoring to ensure that risk controls are implemented and are effective;
(e)   effective communication of information on health and safety issues;
(f)   periodic performance review and feed back.

17   The provider's safety arrangements should be appropriate to the size of the organisation and the extent of activity programmes offered. There should be a clearly defined chain of responsibility for management of any preventive measures required to ensure participants' safety. The provider will need to control, monitor and review the preventive measures, and the risk assessment they were based on, to make sure they are maintained effectively.

18   Safety arrangements may be very simple in the case of a single operator combining the roles of provider, safety adviser and instructor in one, perhaps little more than an aide memoire or checklist. A large provider with several activity centres would need more comprehensive and formal arrangements, perhaps in the form of detailed instructions backed up by an internal safety auditing system. The licensing authority has to decide if the provider's arrangements are appropriate in each case. It is important that the provider makes sure each safety measure is in place whenever it is needed to ensure participants' safety. Where the provider employs staff, then there must be appropriate consultation with those staff or their representatives on matters relating to health and safety.

Competent persons to advise on safety matters (regulations 6(1)(a)(iv) and 9(1)(c))

19   The licensing authority will satisfy itself that the provider's assessment of risks, identification of the safety measures needed and management arrangements to give effect to these measures, are all based on sound knowledge of hazards and on accepted good practice as to what is reasonably practicable to ensure the safety of participants.

20   The licensing authority will look for evidence that management of safety is in the hands of, or effectively advised by, one or more competent people with sufficient knowledge of safety matters in relation to the facilities for adventure activities covered by the licence. There is no need for a separate appointment of a safety adviser if the provider has the appropriate expertise. People who advise on safety matters may be directors, centre managers, instructors other members of the provider's staff or consultants; the important thing is that they are competent to give advice. Providers should also take heed of the advice of relevant NGBs. The people who advise on the safety management systems (risk assessment and the measures and arrangements arising from it) may be different from those who manage the systems day to day. Different people may advise on different aspects of the systems, as long as someone is able to take an overview of the arrangements for safety.

21   Appendix 2 sets out qualifications available from national awarding bodies that will normally demonstrate competence. The 'technical expert' column will help the licensing authority decide whether a provider has access to competent advice. Experience is also important; a person who holds the right technical qualification but has little practical experience may not be competent to advise. It is possible that someone with extensive relevant practical experience who does not hold the qualification in the matrix may also be competent to advise. A provider who relies on such a person will need to satisfy the licensing authority that the person is competent; the licensing authority will take account of the history of relevant experience and knowledge of relevant guidance material.

Sufficient numbers of competent instructors (regulation 9(1)(b)(i))

22   Providers should provide evidence to the licensing authority that they maintain suitable and sufficient arrangements for the recruitment, training (including induction training) and ongoing development, assessment and management of staff, which ensures that all staff with direct involvement in adventure activities are assigned to duties within their proven competence. Providers should ensure that instructors have the training, experience, personal qualities and communication skills appropriate for ensuring the safety of the participants according to their age and taking account of any special educational needs. Providers may demonstrate the competence of their instructors by externally awarded qualification, local validations, in-house training, experience

or any combination of these. There may be other ways. The licensing authority will accept whichever means a provider chooses, so long as it is satisfied that instructor competence has been demonstrated.

Qualifications

23   The 'group instructor/leader' column in the qualification matrices in Appendix 2 will help the licensing authority decide whether a provider has competent instructors. Holders of the specified qualifications would be technically competent to take charge of, and have responsibility for the safety of, a group of participants during an activity session without direct supervision at a particular hazard level in a wide range of circumstances. The 'hazard levels' in the matrices reflect the progression of potential for harm, by reference to place, time of year, etc. There are clearly other factors that should be taken into account and the licensing authority will use discretion interpreting the matrices. Higher levels of experience or qualifications might be required if, for example, the activity involves novice participants in a high-hazard location, or conducting the activity at night or in the absence of other on-site instructors with greater experience. There may be cases where lower levels of competence would be sufficient and acceptable, for example where the activity is at the margins of the licensing scheme's coverage, where an activity is at a level not catered for by a nationally available qualification; or where a well-controlled limited site or route is used frequently. In these cases, the licence will include a condition restricting it to the marginal activity, the limited level or site.

24   The activity may require competences that can be demonstrated by alternative qualifications. For example, a caving qualification may be as appropriate as a climbing one for activities like gorge walking or ghyll scrambling. The activity may require competences that cannot be demonstrated by a single qualification. For example, providers of pony trekking would have to show their instructor/leaders are competent to deal with risks arising from being in rugged and remote country as well as those from the use of horses.

25   Some qualifications require periodic revalidation, are site-specific or have other endorsements. Providers should be able to demonstrate that they have arrangements to assure themselves that instructors have the qualifications they claim and that those held by individuals are valid. The provider should also ensure that staff possess the technical competences required which cannot be demonstrated by national qualifications; for example appropriate experience of the particular operating areas and any specialist equipment used.

Equivalent qualifications

26   The licensing authority will accept other qualifications if the provider can show they are accepted by the NGBs as setting equivalent standards of competence for the particular activity. For example, National Vocational Qualifications, Scottish Vocational Qualifications or other awards developed after the publication of this document; qualifications awarded by bodies in European or other nations; or qualifications particular to specific locations or activities, might all be acceptable.

In-house training

27   Where in-house training, rather than an externally assessed qualification, is the means by which the level of competence specified is assured, the training syllabus should be specified by, and the competence of trained staff assessed by, someone with the competencies to fulfil these roles for the equivalent national

qualification. For transferable qualifications, eg most NGB qualifications, it is good practice for someone other than the trainer to do the assessment.

Competence through experience

28   Where a provider wants to use instructors/leaders whose competence comes through experience, the provider would need to provide evidence acceptable to the licensing authority that their competence is adequate for the task. Evidence that someone with the qualifications to fulfil this role for the equivalent national qualification has assessed their competence would generally be suitable.

Instructor/participant ratios

29   Providers should specify the maximum number of participants they will accept per group instructor/leader and any arrangement they have to vary the number in the light of differing conditions and/or the capabilities of the participants. Relevant guidance from NGBs should be taken into account. Instructor/participant ratios should be consistent with the factors identified through risk assessment including the hazard level of the activity; the ages, abilities and competence of participants; and the experience and competence of the instructor. Accompanying adults may also be taken into account for their contribution to pastoral care, particularly if the party includes young people with special educational needs. However, any accompanying adults participating in activities are to be included in the instructor/participant ratio and are not additional to it.

30   Risk assessment may also identify the need for one or more assistants to the group instructor/leader if the safety of participants is to be ensured; for example if the group instructor/leader would need help in the event of an accident or emergency or to keep the group together. Any assistants should be under the direction of the group instructor/leader and be competent to carry out the delegated responsibilities under the group instructor/leader's direct supervision.

Supervision of novices

31   The age and experience of groups of younger or novice participants should be taken into consideration when determining appropriate supervision arrangements.

Supervision of unaccompanied groups

32   Where older or more experienced participants are allowed to take a higher level of responsibility or a leadership role (for example helming a yacht, leading a rock-climb or conducting an unsupervised expedition in remote country) the provider should:

(a)   have procedures to ensure that the instructor has personal knowledge that the participants are sufficiently experienced and competent to undertake the task, and are adequately trained in first aid and emergency procedures;
(b)   clearly explain the limits of the areas of operation;
(c)   define individual responsibilities; and
(d)   check that the participants have understood these arrangements before they set out.

33   The provider should have a suitable back-up and monitoring system in place while such activities are in progress and which can respond to changes in plan. The authorising and supervision of participant-led activity may require a higher

level of competence and experience than would be acceptable for a group instructor/leader accompanying the group. The licensing authority will consider the circumstances of each application and attach a non-standard condition to the licence if appropriate.

Safety information (regulation 9(1)(b)(ii))

34   Providers will need to demonstrate that they have procedures to ensure that staff and participants are given, in a comprehensible and relevant form, the information they need about the provider's safety measures and arrangements. In particular, participants should be briefed on the correct use of any personal safety equipment, eg buoyancy aids or harnesses, and any other appropriate safety procedures. For expeditions, participants should be briefed on all safety aspects of the journey. Arrangements should cover staff checks that participants have understood the information essential to their safety. Special arrangements may be needed for participants with special educational needs.

35   Providers should have arrangements for defining an operating area for each activity session, appropriate to the level of ability of the group. This may be defined in terms of an identifiable area of water, a particular crag or the start, intermediate and finish points of a journey. This information and estimated timings should be recorded in advance of the session, so that a search area can be defined in the event of an emergency. Any changes of plan should be notified to the holder of such information if possible or catered for in the emergency arrangements.

Equipment (regulation 9(1)(b)(iii))

36   Providers should demonstrate that sufficient personal and other safety equipment, appropriate to the activity and the person, is available for use by participants. The provider should have arrangements to check it is well maintained, fit for the purpose intended, correctly sized and correctly fitted at the start of each session and checked appropriately during the session. Where applicable, equipment should meet the appropriate national, European or international standard.

37   For water activities, personal buoyancy, of a suitable type and size, should be provided for all participants. All craft should have adequate inherent or securely attached buoyancy where it is practicable (exceptions may include improvised rafts, keelboats and cabin-yachts). This should be sufficient to ensure that the craft supports the given number of occupants in the event of capsize or inversion.

38   For mountaineering equipment, which is also commonly used for caving, UIAA (Union International des Associations d'Alpinisme) and EN standards are appropriate.

Maintenance (regulation 9(1)(b)(iv))

39   Providers should have arrangements to ensure equipment used by participants is subject to appropriately frequent checks and the results are recorded. Manufacturers' or suppliers' recommendations for maintenance should be taken account of. Before each use, equipment should be checked to ensure it is safe to use. There should be a system for identifying and, if appropriate, destroying equipment which has been withdrawn as not safe to use.

First aid and emergencies (regulation 9(1)(b)(v))

40   Providers should ensure that all participants are accompanied by, or have ready access to, at least one responsible person with a valid, nationally recognised appropriate first-aid qualification. Most NGB qualifications require the holder to have a current first-aid certificate for the qualification to be valid. Where groups are unaccompanied in the field, at least one member of each group should be trained in emergency procedures and carry appropriate equipment.

41   Providers should have criteria for abandonment or modification of activities to ensure the well-being of participants and their withdrawal to safety in the event of bad or deteriorating conditions. Providers should also maintain written procedures for accidents and emergencies.

42   Providers' emergency arrangements for water activities should be designed to allow the recovery of participants from the water before their life is threatened. In particular, where the activity creates a risk that participants could be unconscious and face down in the water, the emergency arrangements should be designed to allow for their recovery and the immediate start of resuscitation within three minutes of their immersion. For canoeing and sailing in larger craft, a competent instructor with suitable equipment to hand might meet this requirement if instructor/participant ratios are sufficient to ensure the safety of the rest of the group meantime. For dinghy sailing and windsurfing, this will usually involve the provision of one or more immediately available, suitably crewed, powered rescue craft. Where outboard engines power such craft there should be a device to cut out the engine if the helmsman falls overboard while the craft is in motion. Helms of powered rescue craft should hold a Royal Yachting Association (RYA) Level 2 Powerboat award and RYA Safety Boat award or equivalent qualifications, and have adequate experience and training in rescuing the relevant craft.

43   Providers' emergency arrangements for land-based activities should not rely solely on mobile telephones or radios to call for assistance unless the operating area and foreseeable deviations from it are proven to be free of any blind spots where they might not work. Where they are to be used, they should be maintained in good working order and protected from loss or damage.

44   Where activities take place on the sea or some large inland waters, a VHF radio is the most appropriate means of communication in an emergency. Providers will also have to comply with the other relevant legal provisions relating to the use of VHF radios.

45   Providers must have a system for recording and, where required, reporting accidents and dangerous occurrences integrated with their safety management systems. An accident or dangerous occurrence should prompt a review of the risk assessment together with action to prevent recurrences, where appropriate, and should comply with statutory reporting requirements. It is good safety management practice to record and investigate near-miss incidents as these can provide valuable information that can help in preventing an actual accident or dangerous occurrence happening.

Guidance

Guidance on the licensing authority's functions

Application for a licence

46 The purpose of the application is to:

(a) set out what the applicant wants a licence to cover;

(b) allow the licensing authority to judge when an inspection should take place and which authorised person should carry out the inspection; and

(d) allow the authorised person to prepare for an inspection.

47 The licensing authority will provide the following information to providers who enquire about obtaining, renewing or changing a licence:

(a) the form of the application and the documents that the applicant needs to submit with the application;

(b) the fee payment arrangements;

(c) the arrangements for inspection, including what the inspector may wish to see on site;

(d) an outline of the legal requirements and the applicant's rights of representation and appeal;

(e) a list of relevant further guidance literature, with particulars of where it can be obtained.

48 Regulation 4(a) requires applications to be in a form and manner approved by the licensing authority. The licensing authority will provide paper forms or accept electronic equivalents. The application should include the following particulars:

(a) name, postal address and telephone number of the applicant;

(b) the name of a contact person;

(c) the name, postal address and telephone number of the activity centre or operating base, if it is different from the applicant's address;

(d) the nature of the operation to which the application relates:
  (i) its operating season;
  (ii) its purpose (eg multi-activity holidays, education, specialist instruction);

(e) for each adventure activity for which the licence is sought:
  (i) the location(s), site(s) or area(s) to be used;
  (ii) the hazard level(s) of the activity:
  (iii) any restrictions on when the activity is offered during the year;
  (iv) age groups of participants catered for;
  (v) any restriction on participation by children/young people with special educational needs;
  (vi) number of instructors (group instructor/leaders or assistants) engaged or expected to be engaged;
  (vii) particulars of qualifications (or alternative evidence) held, or the minimum required to be held, by instructors;
  (viii) name(s) of technical expert(s) (who may be the applicant), particulars of experience and awards held and where the expert can be contacted;

(f) any restrictions on when the applicant's base or activity sites are available for inspection.

Supporting documentation

49 The licensing authority must specify which documents (or extracts from them) are to accompany applications. It will need evidence of:

(a) assessment of risks to participants;

(b) measures identified to reduce the significant risks;

(c) arrangements made to give continued effect to these measures as set out in guidance on safety standards above.

50   For renewals, it would be acceptable for providers to confirm in writing that the documents supplied with a previous application have not been changed.

51   The licensing authority can refuse to consider an application if it is not in the correct form. Any obvious shortcomings in the adequacy of the information will be drawn to the attention of the applicant so they can be remedied. If shortcomings in the application are not remedied, the licensing authority can refuse to consider the application. Applications will be processed quickly enough to allow a decision to be reached within three months of receipt. Where an applicant is unable to provide access for inspection of equipment or places to be used for adventure activities that would allow a decision to be made within three months, the licensing authority can refuse to consider the application until access is available. If the authority fails to reach a decision within three months of receiving a valid application, a provider may appeal as if against a refusal.

52   The particulars in the application will be used as the basis for arranging an inspection. A large centre offering a wide range of activities at advanced levels may need more than one person and may need more than one visit to inspect. The assigned inspector(s) should read the material submitted with the application in advance of the inspection. Where individuals' qualifications are notified with the application, any checks that the licensing authority wishes to make with awarding bodies should be carried out beforehand to save time during inspection.

53   In the case of an application for the renewal of a licence, the licensing authority may rely upon a report of an inspection made in respect of the licence within a period of one year before the date due for the renewal of the licence.

54   It is an offence for any person who is required to hold a licence to provide activities within the scope of the Regulations without holding a valid licence.

Appointments of inspectors and other persons

55   Regulation 12 allows the licensing authority to authorise suitably experienced or qualified people to make reports to the authority. Such authorisations will be in writing to named individuals and will set out the limits of any delegated functions, including any restriction of time, geographical area, activity or activity hazard level. The document will be shown to anyone who asks to see it.

56   The licensing authority will also appoint, in writing, its directors, employees or persons who are to exercise other statutory functions on its behalf. The appointments will set out any limits of the functions delegated. Those who are appointed to sign documents notifying the licensing authority's decisions to grant, refuse or revoke licences are the Chairman, Chief Executive Officer and the Head of Inspection of AALS.

Competence of inspectors

57   The licensing authority should have an inspectorate with expertise to advise it on the full range of adventure activities, hazard levels and regional environments covered by the licensing scheme and in the inspection and interpretation of safety legislation. The licensing authority will select people with appropriate experience

and qualifications and give them any necessary training before authorising them to carry out inspections.

58   Those carrying out inspections should generally have the qualifications and experience necessary to qualify as technical expert (see Appendix 2) in one or more of the activities prescribed in the Regulations and should have experience of the provision of adventure activities to young persons. They should also be competent in inspection and safety management assessment; people with considerable expertise in these aspects and suitable training in adventure activities could also be appointed as inspectors, particularly for providers with extensive management systems. They should be familiar with relevant general health and safety legislation; the Activity Centres (Young Persons' Safety) Act 1995; the Adventure Activities Licensing Regulations 2004 and other relevant guidance. They must not have any financial or other direct interest in any provider they are assigned to inspect.

59   The licensing authority will make arrangements to monitor the consistency of approach to inspections and to identify needs for and deliver refresher training.

Arranging inspections

60   Except for spot checks, inspections should generally be arranged in advance so that the applicant and any safety adviser the applicant wishes can be present. When the appointment is made, the provider should be given an estimate of the time the inspection might take. They should also be told that length of inspection time does not affect licence fee costs. The fee structure means the provider is not charged by the hour for time spent on site. The licence fee subsumes, in one fee and one payment, the application and inspection fees, which were payable separately under the 1996 Regulations. In the case of a licence renewal where inspection precedes the application, the licensing authority will inform the provider the licence fee will not be due until the provider applies for renewal.

61   Other inspections of licence-holders' activities can be done at any reasonable time, including any time when participants are engaging in adventure activities. The provider's application should include information on the operating season. If considered necessary to make a spot check on a particular activity, a non-standard condition could be included in a licence to require the provider to notify the licensing authority in advance when that activity is programmed.

Conduct of inspections

62   Before deciding whether to issue a licence, the licensing authority has to consider the application in relation to the requirements related to safety set out in regulation 6(1) (including those in regulation 9(1)(a) and (b)). It will need a report that includes advice on:

(a)   whether the applicant satisfies the Regulations;
(b)   whether a licence should be granted or refused;
(c)   the length of the period the licence should remain in force;
(d)   whether it would be appropriate to restrict what the applicant asked for; and
(e)   whether any non-standard safety condition should be included in a licence.

63   Any obvious shortcomings in the adequacy of the proposed provision of activities will be drawn to the attention of the applicant so that they can be remedied.

64   The Authority's report to the provider, together with its decision as to whether to issue a licence, may be based wholly or in part on this report.

65   Inspections should be targeted at what a provider does that gives rise to the most serious risks or where hazards are least well controlled. The primary purpose of the inspection should be to enable a judgement to be made on how well the provider is really managing safety – whether or not they understand the principles and whether the systems described in the application work in practice, so that the inspector can have confidence that standards will stay acceptable even when the inspector is not there. Equipment and personnel checks alone will only show that standards are right on that day so emphasis should be placed on proper safety management of the activities.

66   Information should be gathered from people about what they know and what they do and then be corroborated by reference to evident physical conditions and any relevant paperwork systems. This means that management staff will always need to be interviewed. Equipment used for activities, places to be used for activities and instructors should also be sampled during inspection visits, wherever possible while activities are in progress. The mix and depth of inspection can be varied so long as enough information is gathered to form a valid view about the management systems.

67   The inspector should visit the places specified for adventure activities if that is necessary to enable a judgement to be made on the provider's safety management systems. This is likely to be necessary when the provider's safety arrangements are tailored for a particular location and instructors are purpose trained in-house for that location. Such a visit may not be necessary if the provider's systems and the instructors' competence are clearly designed to cater appropriately for the activity at high hazard levels over a wide range of locations and climatic conditions, for example in the case of a specialist mountain guide or peripatetic canoeing instructor.

68   Wherever possible, the inspector should ask group instructors/leaders and their assistants questions to assess their technical competence and knowledge of what they need to know of the provider's arrangements on, for example, first aid and emergency arrangements. The inspector should also examine randomly selected equipment and related maintenance records. The inspector may also wish to speak to participants to assess how well relevant information is communicated to them.

69   In some cases, the applicant may not be able to demonstrate the effectiveness of all the management systems that need to be checked. This is likely to be the case for any new provider getting a licence to start up and providers of 'summer camps' or other restricted season facilities. If the licensing authority is satisfied that the provider's management systems are generally appropriate but considers further checks are needed to give confidence, the licensing authority will consider issuing a licence with non-standard conditions, for example requiring notice of when the facilities are available for full inspection or requiring submission of further particulars.

Frequency of inspections and period of validity of licences

70   The licensing authority will have a rating system for determining the interval between planned full inspections. It will set the expiry date of licences to achieve this, and no license will exceed the overall maximum of three years (regulation 8(d)).

71   Where there are pressures on the safety management system, inspections should be more frequent. Advice on license duration should form part of the inspection report. The prioritisation system should rate the following factors and assign a licence duration according to the overall score:

Guidance

(a) number and vulnerability of participants at risk;

(b) number and type of activities offered;

(c) turnover of staff;

(d) pressure on in-house training provision;

(e) arrangements depending on temporary facilities;

(d) the provider's track record, including complaints investigated and found to be justified.

72   In general, activity centres catering for large numbers of participants on multi-activity packages depending on seasonal part-time, purpose-trained staff should be inspected at least annually. Large activity centres with permanent establishments and staff should be inspected at least every second year. Where there is a substantial overlap with a NGB centre inspection scheme, the licensing authority will take that into account in determining the licence duration. The maximum three-year interval between licensing inspections should be reserved for providers with stable and robust safety management systems and a settled, highly competent staff.

73   In addition to full inspections relating to applications, the licensing authority will also arrange a programme of random spot-check inspections, with or without notice, of a proportion of licence-holders. Providers will not be charged a separate fee for these inspections as the licence fee includes a provision for them.

Exercise of discretion in relation to standards

74   The licensing authority will use discretion in reaching decisions. It has choices in the sanctions it can impose to eliminate the unsafe and promote the safe. It can refuse a licence or it can issue one with restricting non-standard conditions. It can also adopt other approaches, such as giving advice on good practice, that can often be effective in promoting good standards of safety.

75   Discretion is needed in deciding whether providers have met safety standards. The licensing authority will use its powers to require measures that are reasonably practicable for the provider to take to secure the safety of participants. That means that where standards are not specified in guidance, the licensing authority must always take account of cost as well as the degree of risk. The licensing authority expects that relevant good practice will be followed. Where relevant good practice in particular cases is not clearly established, for example where there is no relevant NGB, the significance of the risks (both their extent and likelihood) will be assessed to determine what action needs to be taken. Some irreducible risks may be so serious that the activity cannot be permitted. At the other extreme, some risks may be so minimal that it is not worth spending more resources to reduce them. The licensing authority will require providers to take measures to reduce risk, so far as is reasonably practicable, bearing in mind the intended benefit of the adventurous activity.

76   The licensing authority will develop and publish criteria, based on this guidance, which it will use in reaching its decisions. It will work constructively with NGBs and other appropriate bodies to do so and to develop all necessary safety standards for activities covered by the licensing scheme.

77   Provided participant's safety is ensured, the licensing authority will not refuse a licence on grounds solely related to the quality of the coaching or teaching given to participants.

Licences

78   The licence issued to the licence-holder will be on paper, which allows the licence-holder to photocopy the writing but also allows the original licence to be readily identifiable, for example, by watermark or the like. It should include the name, address and telephone number and e-mail address where people can direct enquiries and complaints. Every licence must include the standard licence conditions set out in regulation 9(1)(a)–(g). They place duties on the provider to give effect to the requirements related to safety, to co-operate with the licensing authority by allowing inspections and giving information and to make the licence available for inspection by the public.

79   The standard licence condition in regulation 9(1)(g) requires the licence holder to state in any advertising material what activities are covered by the licence and how to contact the licensing authority. The licensing authority will provide licence holders with a standard format for this.

80   Unless the provider has satisfied the licensing authority on the full range of possible activities within the definition of an adventure activity (regulation 2(1)), the licence should include, in addition to the standard conditions, non-standard conditions that specify:

(a)   the activity covered;
(b)   the upper hazard levels within the activity;
(c)   the geographical area; and/or
(d)   the time of year of operations.

81   If the application relates to an activity centre, the licence should also include the name and address of the centre covered by the licence.

82   Regulation 9(2) allows the licensing authority to attach further non-standard licence conditions provided they are necessary for safety.

Notifications – rights of representation and appeal

83   In serving notice of its decisions, the licensing authority must adopt procedures that meet the Schedule to the Regulations. This requires the licensing authority to give the provider time to object before any non-standard condition takes effect or a licence is refused or revoked. If the provider wishes to object or make representations at this stage then they should follow the procedure AALA has established. Details of this procedure will always be given to applicants when they are notified of the authority's intentions. Every effort will be made to achieve a mutually acceptable satisfactory outcome.

84   If the licensing authority is aware of a risk of injury that is a matter of evident concern, ie a situation where the licensing authority considers that the risk is so serious or so likely that it warrants short-term action to control it, then it will alert the relevant enforcing authority to the matter as quickly as reasonably possible.

85   At the end of an inspection, the findings of the inspection and what the inspector intends to give as advice to the licensing authority will be discussed with the provider. In particular, if a recommendation of refusal of the licence application or the imposition of restrictive licence conditions, the provider will be told of this with the reasons why. The provider will be given the opportunity to correct any errors of fact or misunderstandings that may have been used in arriving at that recommendation.

86   If, after the procedures detailed in paragraph 83 have been followed, the authority decides to refuse to issue a licence, to impose non-standard conditions, to vary or refuse to grant a requested variation to an existing licence or decides to revoke a licence, the provider, or applicant as appropriate, has a right of appeal to the Relevant National Authority. Relevant National Authority means, in relation to England and Scotland, the Secretary of State and in relation to Wales, the National Assembly for Wales. In the event that the authority is proposing to take any of the actions above, then information about the right of appeal will be provided to the applicant or provider.

Making information public

87   Schools and parents, as well as providers, need to know about the licensing scheme. The licensing authority will take steps to publicise its activities – the requirement for a licence, what a licence covers and other matters which could include the differences between the statutory and any relevant voluntary schemes.

88   To meet the requirement for a publicly accessible register of licence holders (regulation 13), the licensing authority will ensure that its register is kept up to date. Particulars of applicants who have been refused a licence will be recorded but will not be held on the public register.

89   The purpose of the register is to allow interested parties to quickly and easily find out which providers hold a licence. The absence of a provider of adventurous activities from the register does not necessarily mean that they are operating illegally; they may simply not be within scope of the scheme.

90   Inspection reports will be copied to the provider unless there are legal constraints such as pending consideration of enforcement action. Inspection reports on which decisions to grant licences were based will also be made available to members of the public who ask for them, subject to freedom of information and data protection legislation. The licensing authority will consider every request on its individual merits, taking advice as necessary.

Investigation of complaints

91   The licensing authority has to consider any complaints about the safety standards in relation to licence holders but if the complaint does not relate to facilities for adventure activities within its remit, the licensing authority will pass the complaint on to the appropriate enforcing authority and provide assistance to the enforcing authority where required. The licensing authority will investigate appropriately all complaints within its remit. It will always tell the complainant the results of any investigation and what it has done. This function is generally carried out by the licensing service on behalf of the licensing authority.

Liaison with enforcing authorities

92   The licensing authority will co-operate with other health and safety enforcing authorities (local authorities). A memorandum of understanding will be agreed between them setting out the detail of areas of responsibility; avoidance of overlap; liaison arrangements and arrangements for speedy contact in cases where there is evidence of matters of serious concern. Where, in the course of their inspections, the licensing authority inspectors become aware of serious shortcomings in matters outside the scope of the licensing scheme, then they will draw these concerns to the attention of the appropriate enforcing authorities responsible for health and safety, fire or other legislation.

Reports to the Health and Safety Commission

93   The licensing authority has to provide annual reports to the Health and Safety Commission and to the relevant national authority – that is, the Secretary of State (in relation to England and Scotland) and the Welsh Assembly Government (in relation to Wales). As a matter of courtesy, the report will also be copied to the Scottish Parliament. The report will include:

(a)   the number of inspections;
(b)   the number of inspector days spent on inspections related to the issue or renewal of a licence and on other inspections;
(c)   the number of licences granted, varied and refused including the reasons for refusal.

Payment of fees

94   The full fee must accompany applications. If the full fee is not received, the licensing authority will not grant a licence or a renewal.

Appendix 1

Further information and interpretation

Introduction

1   The notes in this Appendix will assist providers in deciding whether or not they need a licence. They do not replace the Regulations and ultimately only the courts can decide the effect of the Regulations.

2   Regulation 2(1) gives precise meaning for many of the words and expressions as they are to be used in the Regulations. In what follows, words in *italics* are defined in regulation 2(1).

3   Regulation 3 sets out who is required to hold a licence. The overall effect is that anyone who provides *facilities for adventure activities* must have a licence if the provision is in return for payment or by a local authority to a school or college and the provision is not within one of the exempted categories in regulation 3(2).

Facilities for adventure activities

4   '*Facilities for adventure activities*', the provision of which is subject to licensing, is defined in regulation 2(1) as 'any facilities which consist of, or include some element of, instruction or leadership given to one or more *young persons* in connection with their engagement in an *adventure activity* (other than instructions given solely in connection with the supply of equipment for use in such an activity).' The provider giving instruction as described in the bracket would, however, still be subject to the Health and Safety at Work etc Act 1974 and the Management of Health and Safety at Work Regulations 1999 and would be required to have appropriate safety management systems in place. Where the licensing authority has concerns about the safety of the equipment hired or about the activities of a provider in this category, it will inform the appropriate enforcing authority. There is no requirement to hold a licence if there is no instruction or leadership provided or if the people engaging in the activity are all aged 18 years or more.

5   '*Adventure activity*' is defined in regulation 2(1) as '*caving, climbing, trekking or watersports*' and each of these is defined in detail in regulation 2(1). In the case of trekking and watersports, some words used in the definitions *(horse, skiing, moorland, travelling time, accessible road, refuge* and *specified waters)* are further defined. There is no need for a licence for any activity that is not covered by the definitions in the Regulations.

6   The Activity Centres (Young Persons' Safety) Act 1995 does not extend beyond Great Britain (England, Scotland and Wales and their territorial waters), so any adventure activity carried out in Northern Ireland, the Isle of Man, the Channel Islands or elsewhere outside Great Britain is not subject to this licensing regime.

The 'person' who is required to hold a licence

7   Regulation 3 sets out who needs to hold a licence and who does not.

8   A person is required to hold a licence if that person receives payment for *facilities for adventure activities*. In law, a 'person' need not be an individual; it can also be a body of persons, corporate or unincorporate. Local authorities, limited companies, partnerships, trusts, societies and clubs are all persons.

9   The payment relates to *facilities for adventure activities*, not only to the instruction or leadership element of the facilities. A licence would still be required even if the instruction or leadership element is nominally free but not available to people who have not paid for transport, catering, accommodation or some other part of a provider's package.

10   A local authority will need a licence for the *facilities for adventure activities* it offers in return for payment in the same way as other providers. In addition, regulation 3(1)(b) means that a local authority is required to hold a licence if it provides facilities to *educational establishments* (schools, colleges etc) for their pupils without requiring payment. Local authorities do not require to hold a licence for any other *facilities for adventure activities* they provide free.

11   The Activity Centres (Young Persons' Safety) Act 1995 does not extend to the Crown so the Regulations do not place any obligations to hold a licence on the Crown, or on Crown servants providing facilities for adventure activities in the due course of their duties. Cadet force officers are Crown servants while on duty.

12   Regulation 3(2) exempts a number of specific cases from the general requirement to hold a licence:

(a)   A *voluntary association* (a non-profit making membership organisation) does not require a licence to provide facilities to its own members or, by arrangement, to the members of another *voluntary association*. They can also hold open days or taster events to interest members of the public in their activities or to attract new members so long as no individual non-member participates in this way for more than three days in any period of a year. People made temporary members for the duration of a course or series of sessions sold by the association are not considered to be members for the purposes of the licensing scheme. A voluntary association selling facilities to the general public or to a school is required to hold a licence.

(b)   An *educational establishment* (a school, college or university) does not require a licence for provision to its own pupils or students. They do require a licence for provision to pupils of another educational establishment or to other members of the public, when provided in return for payment. Activity centres, field studies centres and other outdoor education centres run by education authorities or departments are excluded from the definition of an *educational establishment* and so are required to have a licence. Other provision by education authorities or departments is treated in the same way as any other local authority provision.

13   An *educational establishment* is not required to hold a licence if it provides otherwise in-scope adventure activities to its own pupils engaged in a Duke of Edinburgh's Award (or similar). Special consideration may be given to young persons who have left school the previous term, and who wish to continue participating in the school's Duke of Edinburgh programme without the school being required to hold a licence.

14   A licence is not required by anyone who provides activities only to family groups where the young people are each accompanied during the activity by an individual who is their own parent or a legally appointed individual guardian. It would be reasonable to expect the parent or legally appointed guardian to be within sight and sound of the young person taking part in the activity. This exemption does not extend to relationships 'in loco parentis' such as school teachers, social workers or youth leaders.

15   A licensable provider must hold a licence before offering licensable activities. Providers who do not offer licensable activities (for example those who offer activities only to people aged 18 or over or whose activities do not involve an element of instruction or leadership) are not required to hold a licence. The licensing authority will assist providers to determine if their status or provision requires them to hold a licence but will not charge for this assistance.

16   Where someone wishes to provide licensable activities they must apply for a licence before those activities commence and the licensing authority may inspect the provider's overall safety management as it relates to licensable activities (for example, of equipment, staffing and paperwork) and, if satisfied, grant a licence.

17   The licensing authority has no power under the Regulations to inspect a provider whom it thinks might require a licence but has not applied for one. The licensing authority may offer advice and assistance to the provider to determine licensable status. If the provider declines the offer and the licensing authority still has concerns then it should report this to the appropriate enforcing authority.

18   If one person holds a licence, another person does not need to hold a licence for the same facilities even if that other person receives payment for it. If a hotel or other agency takes bookings from its clients for activity sessions provided by a licence holder, the hotel would not require to hold a licence. It would require a licence if it used an unlicensed provider.

Licences for *activity centre* based providers

19   The requirement to hold a licence does not depend on whether or not the provider operates an *activity centre*. The term *activity centre* is used in the Regulations only to determine cases where more than one licence must be held by a single provider and also for certain requirements relating to a licence.

20   *Activity centre* is defined in regulation 2 as an establishment which is, at the time in question, primarily used for, or as a base for, the provision of instruction or leadership in sporting, recreational or outdoor activities. If a person operates more than one *activity centre* at the same time throughout any period of at least 28 days, a separate licence is required for each centre at or from which *facilities for adventure activities* are provided at any time during that period. An *activity centre* that sometimes caters for young people and sometimes for adults is still an *activity centre* for this purpose so long as the same person operates it for at least 28 consecutive days. One licence can cover the *facilities for adventure activities* provided from several centres run simultaneously during a period shorter than 28 days. One licence can also cover operations run consecutively from a series of temporary centres.

Definitions of activities

Caving

21   *Caving* for the purposes of the licensing scheme covers most activities done underground in natural caves or in mines, including variants described as potholing, cave diving and mine exploration. It does not include visits to the parts of show caves or tourist mines that are open to the public or to the parts of the mines (underground excavations made for the purpose of getting minerals) that are still being worked. It also excludes visits to natural caves or parts of caves that give rise only to everyday hazards that would be obvious to and surmountable by someone with no previous experience of the cave or special knowledge of hazards in caves. A judgement on whether exploration can be carried out safely without

the application of special skills or techniques may have to be made by an expert in caving except in the most straightforward of cases. A licence would always be needed if rock climbing or diving equipment were required for safe access.

Climbing

22   *Climbing* for the purposes of the licensing scheme covers most activities involving movement over difficult terrain that requires the use of hands as well as feet and where safety requires either the use of the equipment or the skills and techniques of a rock or ice climber. As well as rock climbing and ice climbing it includes variants such as gorge walking, ghyll scrambling and sea-level traversing. A licence is not required for scrambling where injury would not occur if equipment or special techniques to protect the individual from falling were not used and where other hazards that might cause injury are everyday hazards that would be obvious to and surmountable by someone with no previous experience of rock or ice climbing. Use of climbing walls, abseiling towers and similar man-made structures designed for practising climbing techniques are excluded from licensing but this does not extend to other outdoor man-made structures such as disused railway viaducts.

Trekking

23   *Trekking* for the purposes of the licensing scheme covers walking, pony trekking, mountain biking, off-piste skiing, or similar, in remote open country. Travelling in any place which is *moorland* (open uncultivated land at any height above sea level) or on a mountain above 600 m and from which it would take more than 30 minutes *travelling time*, using the standard Naismith's Rule, to walk back to an *accessible road* or *refuge* is subject to licensing except for on-piste *skiing*. Journeys by public transport or other mechanised means are not subject to licensing.

24   Woodland, forests and other cultivated land is excluded from the definition only where it is less than 600 m above sea level. A road that does not have the width or surface to be used by an ordinary road-going ambulance would not be an *accessible road*. A *refuge* is a building offering shelter for the party in an emergency and it must either be occupied or have some means of summoning help. The distance that can be covered in the 30 minutes *travelling time* will never be more than 2.5 km and will be less if there are uphill sections on the route back. It must also be over a route that can be walked safely so must not have any unfordable rivers or precipitous ground on it. Time of year and weather conditions may mean that a road is not an *accessible road* or a seasonally open or occupied building is not a *refuge* at some times of the year. The distance calculated by reference to *travelling time* is a standard one not dependent on weather conditions or the capabilities of the party that might require the adoption of a smaller distance.

25   Within the remote areas described in paragraph 24, any activity that involves journeying on foot, on *horse* (includes pony) or on pedal cycle or *skiing* off-piste is subject to licensing. *Skiing* is defined as sliding over snow or ice on skis, skates, sledges or similar equipment (eg snowboards or improvised sledges).

Watersports

26   *Watersports* for the purposes of the licensing scheme covers most activities involving unpowered craft on certain *specified waters*. The *specified waters* include any place within the territorial limits of Great Britain on the sea or any other tidal waters, including estuaries, the tidal reaches of rivers, sea lochs and

harbours. The term also includes any body of inland water in which it is possible to be more than 50 m from the nearest perimeter bank; and any inland waters where the surface is turbulent because of weirs, rapids, waterfalls or fast-flowing currents (white water). A licence is not needed for use of craft on inland lakes, lochs or other bodies of placid water that are less than 100 m wide throughout their length and where surface turbulence is limited to the regular waves produced by wind action. If a lake or loch is greater than 100 m wide, use of craft on any part of that body of water would be subject to licensing; a river or canal connected to it would be a separate body of water or location and would not be subject to licensing unless there is white water there. Any stretch of inland water that is categorised at Grade II or above according to the International Canoe Federation classification would be subject to licensing. Grade 1 waters would normally be outside licensing, but unlicensed providers will not be able to use them when they are turbulent at times of spate flow.

27   The craft subject to licensing, if used on *specified water*s, are canoes, kayaks or similar craft; rafts (inflatable, improvised, rigid, etc); and sailing boats, windsurfers, sailing dinghies or other wind-propelled craft. A licence is not required for the use of rowing boats, powered or towed inflatables or rafts, and the larger sailing vessels that go to sea and are subject to Merchant Shipping Act certification.

Appendix 2

Technical competence – qualification matrices

1 These matrices should be interpreted in conjunction with paragraphs 23-28 of this guidance and with the guidance relating to the qualifications published by the bodies that award them.

2 Other acceptable qualifications may be devised following publication of this guidance and the licensing authority will form a judgement on the acceptability of them.

Abbreviations used in the matrices

ABRS	Association of British Riding Schools
BASI	British Association of Snowsport Instructors
BCA	British Caving Association
BCU	British Canoe Union
BHS	British Horse Society
BMG	British Association of Mountain Guides
BOB	British Off-road Biking
CCPR	Central Council of Physical Recreation
CIC	Cave Instructor Certificate
CWA	Climbing Wall Award
ESC	English Ski Council
LCMLA	Local Cave and Mine Leader Assessment Scheme (BCA)
MIA	Mountain Instructor Award (MLTUK)
MIAS	Mountain-bike Instructors Award Scheme
MIC	Mountain Instructor Certificate (MLTUK)
ML	Mountain Leader
MLA	Mountain Leader Award (MLTUK)
MLTS	Mountain Leader Training Scotland
MLTUK	Mountain Leader Training UK
MLTW	Mountain Leader Training Wales
NVQ	National Vocational Qualifications
OTC	Off-road Training Consultancy
RYA	Royal Yachting Association
SCOW	Ski Council of Wales
SI	Senior Instructor (RYA)
SMBLA	Scottish Mountain Bike Leaders Award
SNSC	Scottish National Ski Council
SPA	Single Pitch Award (MLTB)
SRA	Scottish Rafting Association
SVQ	Scottish Vocational Qualifications
TRSS	Trekking and Riding Society of Scotland
UKCC	UK Coaching Certificate
WGL	Walking Group Leader Award
WTRA	Welsh Trekking and Riding Association

Caving
(See Appendix 1, paragraph 21)

Hazard level	Group instructor/leader	Technical expert
Cave/mine systems with pitches over 18 m	CIC holder (or S/NVQ Level 4)	CIC holder (or S/NVQ Level 4)
Cave/mine systems with pitches less than 18 m	As above, or LCMLA Level 2 (or S/NVQ Level 3)	As above
Cave/mine system without pitches	As above, or LCMLA Level 1 (or S/NVQ Level 2)	As above
Show cave/tourist mines – adventure trips beyond public areas with made-up lit paths	As above, depending on level of activity	As above

Climbing
(See Appendix 1, paragraph 22)

Hazard level	Group instructor/leader	Technical expert
Winter climbing	MIC or BMG Carnet holder or Aspirant Guide	MIC or BMG Carnet holder
Rock climbing – multipitch	As above, or MIA	As above or MIA
Ghyll scrambling, gorge walking or sea-level traversing	As above, or in-house assessed depending on level of activity	As above
Rock climbing – single pitch	As above, or SPA or Rock Climbing Leader (N Ireland) or in-house assessed	As above
Other climbing, abseiling or scrambling on man-made structures or natural features	As above, or in-house assessed, depending on level of activity. CWA for man-made structures	As above

Notes

1   The above information is based on information extracted from a matrix for Mountaineering in the MLTUK National Guidelines. This embraces both climbing and much of trekking as these terms are defined in the Regulations. In cases of doubt on interpretation, refer to the MLTUK guidelines.

2   'Winter' means when winter conditions, including snow and ice, prevail or are forecast. This cannot be defined by a portion of the year. Summer means any conditions not covered under 'winter'.

3   In-house assessment should be conducted by a technical expert.

Trekking – on foot
(see Appendix 1, paragraphs 23–25)

Hazard level	Group instructor/leader	Technical expert
Mountain country – winter	MIC or BMG Carnet holder or Aspirant Guide or Winter ML. International ML for rolling terrain where crampons and ice axe are not needed by group members	MIC or BMG Carnet holder
Moorland country – winter	MIC or BMG Carnet holder or Aspirant Guide or Winter ML or International Mountain Leader ML for rolling terrain where crampons and ice axe are not needed by group members	As above or IML
Mountain country – summer	As above or MIA or Summer ML or European ML	As above or MIA and Winter ML
Moorland country – summer	As above or WGL	As above or MIA
Lowland country	WGL award	As above or Summer ML

Notes

1   The above information is based on information extracted and updated from a matrix for mountaineering in the MLTUK National Guidelines. This embraces both climbing and much of trekking as these terms are defined in the Regulations. In cases of doubt or interpretation, refer to the MLTUK guidelines.

2   'Winter' means when winter conditions, including snow and ice, prevail or are forecast, this cannot be defined by a portion of the year. Summer means any conditions not covered under 'winter'.

Trekking – on horse
(see Appendix 2, paragraphs 23–25)

Hazard level	Group instructor/leader	Technical expert
Levels as in *Trekking on foot* matrix but when horse riding	The appropriate on-foot qualification plus an appropriate award from one of ABRS, BHS, TRSS or WTRA	The appropriate on-foot qualification plus an appropriate award from one of ABRS, BHS, TRSS or WTRA

Trekking – on pedal cycle
(See Appendix 1, paragraphs 23–25)

Hazard level	Group instructor/leader	Technical expert
Levels as in *Trekking on foot* matrix but when cycling	The appropriate on-foot qualification plus an appropriate award from one of BOB, MIAS, OTC or SMBLA	The appropriate on-foot qualification plus an appropriate award from one of BOB, MIAS, OTC or SMBLA

Note

1   Other local or national schemes may be or become appropriate.

Trekking – off-piste ski touring
(See Appendix 1, paragraphs 23–25)

Hazard level	Group instructor/leader	Technical expert
Ski-mountaineering	BMG Carnet holder or SNSC Mountain Ski Leader	BMG Carnet holder or SNSC Mountain Ski Leader
Alpine skiing – Scotland – off-piste away from marked/serviced areas	As above, or winter ML and one of BASI 2 ski teacher or SNSC APC or SNSC/ESC/SCOW club coach	As above
Alpine skiing – Scotland – off-piste but within the recognised boundary of serviced area shown on piste map	As above, or BASI 2 Ski Teacher or BASI 3 Ski Instructor or SNSC Alpine Ski Leader	As above, or BASI Ski Teacher
Nordic skiing – Scotland – off-piste (away from marked/serviced areas)	Winter ML and one of BASI 3 relevant to discipline or SNSC Nordic Ski Leader, ESC/SCOW Nordic Coach (touring) or ESC/SCOW club coach	BASI 2 Nordic Ski Teacher or SNSC Mountain Ski Leader or Winter ML and ESC/SCOW Nordic Coach (touring)
Nordic or Alpine skiing – England and Wales	As above relevant to discipline for Scotland, or Winter ML, and ESC/SCOW tour leader	As above relevant to discipline for Scotland, or Winter ML, and ESC/SCOW Coach
Snowboarding (Scotland) off-piste	Winter ML and one of BASI Snowboard Teacher or SNSC Snowboard Performance Coach	Winter ML and BASI Snowboard Teacher
Snowboarding (Scotland) off-piste within the boundaries of resort	As above or BASI Snowboard Instructor or SNSC Snowboard Leader	As above plus SNSC Snowboard Performance Coach

Note

1   The above qualifications relate to Nordic and Alpine skiing. Nordic and Alpine refer to the particular ski disciplines, not to geographical settings.

Watersports – canoeing and kayaking
(See Appendix 1, paragraphs 26–27)

Hazard level	Group instructor/leader	Technical expert
Advanced sea	Level 3 Coach (sea) with 5 star (sea)	Level 5 Coach (sea)
Sea – journeys	As above or Level 3 Coach (sea)	As above or Level 3 Coach (sea) with 5 star (sea)
Large lochs – journeys (kayaks only, see below for open canoes)	As above or Level 3 Coach	As above or Level 3 Kayak Coach (inland) with 5 star
Sea and large lochs – activities close to suitable beaches	As above or Level 2 Coach trained for area with relevant 4 star (or appropriate S/NVQ Level 2 Canoeing Coach)	As above or Level 3 (sea) or Level 3 Kayak Coach with 4 star
Sheltered tidal waters	As above or Level 2 Coach (sea) or (appropriate S/NVQ Level 2 Canoeing Coach)	As above
Large lochs – journeys (open canoes)	Level 3 Canoe Coach with 5 star canoe	Level 4 Canoe Coach
Advanced surf (>1 metre)	Level 3 Surf Coach	Level 3 Surf Coach
Surf	As above or Trainee Level 3 Surf Coach	As above or Level 3 Surf Coach
Advanced white water (Grade III and above)	Level 3 Coach with 5 star (inland)	Level 5 Coach
White water (Grade II)	As above, or Level 3 Coach	As above or Level 3 Coach with 5 star (inland)
Sheltered inland water	As above or Level 2 Coach or (appropriate S/NVQ Level 2 Canoeing Coach)	As above or Level 3 Coach

Notes

1   Instructor qualifications referred to above must be relevant to the discipline being delivered, ie canoeing or kayaking.

2   BCU star gradings are given as an indication of the level of competence required, not prerequisites.

3   Surf qualifications are for repeated manoeuvring through waves on recognised surf beaches; sea qualifications cover access through surf for sea journeys etc.

4   White water grades as defined by the International Canoe Federation.

5   The BCU is currently in the process of moving to a system of qualification that is compliant with the UK Coaching Certificate arrangements. This is likely to alter the terms used in the above matrix, in which case the authority will publish a revised matrix. The star awards are also under review and when finalised may require a revision to the above matrix, in which case the authority will publish a revised matrix.

6   Some transferability exists between canoe and kayak awards and may be further developed.

Watersports – rafting
(See Appendix 1, paragraphs 26–27)

Hazard level	Group instructor/leader	Technical expert
White water consistently Grade III and above	Raft Trip Leader	Level 4: Raft Guide Trainer
White water (up to and not exceeding Grade III)	Raft Trip Leader (Restricted)	Level 4: Raft Guide Trainer
Grade I river	Raft Guide (Restricted)	As above
Controlled sites – white water	As above or in-house site specific training	As above

Notes

1   The above qualifications relate to white water rafting using inflatable rafts. At the time of publication, there are no national qualifications for improvised rafts or for inflatable rafts on other waters.

2   'Controlled sites' means short lengths of river, managed and with a safety infrastructure, eg Tryweryn (North Wales), Holme Pierrepont (Nottingham) and Teesside (Cleveland).

3   White water grades as defined by International Canoe Federation.

Watersports – small boat sailing
(See Appendix 1, paragraphs 26–27)

Hazard level	Group instructor/leader	Technical expert
Sea/tidal waters – coastal journeys	Senior Instructor Coastal	Senior Instructor Coastal
Sea/tidal waters – from a harbour or suitable beach	Senior Instructor Coastal (or S/NVQ Level 2 coach)	Senior Instructor Coastal
Inland waters	Instructor Inland (or S/NVQ Level 2 coach)	Senior Instructor Inland

Note

1   Instructor qualifications should be relevant to craft used, ie dinghies or keelboats.

Watersports – windsurfing
(See Appendix 1, paragraphs 26–27)

Hazard level	Group instructor/leader	Technical expert
Sea/tidal waters	Start Windsurfing Instructor Coastal (or S/NVQ Level 2 coach)	Windsurfing Senior Instructor Coastal
Inland waters	As above, Start Windsurfing Instructor Inland (or S/NVQ Level 2 coach)	Windsurfing Senior Instructor Inland

| Appendix 3 | **The Adventure Activities Licensing Regulations 2004** |

| Regulation 1 | **Citation and commencement** |

Regulation 1

These Regulations may be cited as the Adventure Activities Licensing Regulations 2004 and shall come into force on 9 June 2004.

| Regulation 2 | **Interpretation** |

Regulation

(1)   In these Regulations -

"the 1974 Act" means the Health and Safety at Work etc. Act 1974;

"the 1995 Act" means the Activity Centres (Young Persons' Safety) Act 1995;

"the 1996 Regulations" means the Adventure Activities Licensing Regulations 1996[(a)];

"accessible road" means a road which is, at the time in question, accessible to ambulances which are road-going vehicles not specially adapted for rugged terrain;

"activity centre" means an establishment which is, at the time in question, primarily used for, or as a base for, the provision of instruction or leadership in sporting, recreational or outdoor activities;

"adventure activity" means caving, climbing, trekking or watersports;

"caving" means the exploration of underground passages (other than those principally used as show-places open to the public) -

(a)   in parts of mines which are no longer worked; or

(b)   in natural caves where the exploration of those passages requires, in order to be carried out safely, the use of rock climbing or diving equipment or the application of special skills or techniques;

"climbing" means climbing, traversing, abseiling or scrambling over natural terrain or outdoor man-made structures (other than structures designed for such activities) which requires, in order to be carried out safely, the use of equipment for, or the application of special skills or techniques in, rock climbing or ice climbing;

"educational establishment" means an educational establishment attended by young persons except such an establishment engaged primarily in the provision of sporting, recreational or outdoor activities;

"enforcing authority" has the meaning assigned to it by section 18(7) of the 1974 Act;

"facilities for adventure activities" means any facilities which consist of, or include, some element of instruction or leadership given to one or more young persons in connection with their engagement in an adventure activity (other than instructions given solely in connection with the supply of equipment for use in such an activity);

2

"horse" includes pony;

"instructor" means a person giving instruction or leadership in the course of the provision of facilities for adventure activities;

"licence" means a licence granted by the licensing authority in accordance with these Regulations or the 1996 Regulations (whether as a renewal of a licence or otherwise);

"licence-holder" means a person to whom a licence has been granted in accordance with these Regulations or the 1996 Regulations;

"licensing authority" means the person for the time being designated by the Secretary of State or the National Assembly for Wales by order under section 1(1) of the 1995 Act;

"local authority" means -

    (a)   in relation to England, a county council, a unitary authority, a district council, a London borough council, the Common Council of the City of London or the Council of the Isles of Scilly;

    (b)   in relation to Wales, a county council or county borough council; and

    (c)   in relation to Scotland, a council constituted under section 2 of the Local Government etc. (Scotland) Act 1994[b];

"moorland" excludes any woodland or cultivated land;

"non-standard condition" means a condition imposed in a licence other than a condition imposed under regulation 9(1);

"refuge" means a building which would, in an emergency, provide shelter and which was, at the time in question, either occupied or provided with a telephone, or other means of communication, by which help could be summoned;

"relevant national authority" means -

    (a)   in relation to England and Scotland, the Secretary of State;

    (b)   in relation to Wales, the National Assembly for Wales;

"required fee" means (subject to regulation 19) the fee referred to in regulation 5;

"ski-ing" means sliding over snow or ice on skis, skates, sledges or similar equipment;

"specified waters" means -

    (a)   the sea;

    (b)   tidal waters;

    (c)   inland waters at a location where any part of those waters is more than 50 metres from the nearest land excluding any island; or

    (d)   inland waters where the surface of the water is made turbulent because of weirs, rapids, waterfalls or fast flowing currents;

Regulation

"travelling time" means the time it would take a person to walk by the quickest safe route; and for this purpose a person shall be deemed to walk at 5 kilometres per hour and to take, in addition, one minute for every 10 metres of increase in the height above sea level of any uphill section of that route;

"trekking" means journeying on foot, horse or pedal cycle or ski-ing over terrain -

(a) *which is moorland or more than 600 metres above sea level; and*

(b) *from which it would take more than 30 minutes travelling time to reach any accessible road or refuge;*

but does not include ski-ing on a prepared and marked-out ski-run which is patrolled by persons engaged to assist in cases of injury;

"voluntary association" means an association, club, society, organisation or other body (whether corporate or unincorporate) which provides facilities to its members and is not a business, or part of a business, conducted for profit; and "member" in relation to such an association shall exclude a person who is made a member solely in connection with the sale to him by the association of a course of instruction;

"watersports" means the use on specified waters of -

(a) *canoes, kayaks or similar craft propelled or steered by paddles held in the hand (but excluding rowing-boats propelled or steered by oars);*

(b) *rafts (including those which are inflatable or which are improvised from various materials but excluding those propelled by means of a motor or towed by a motor-boat); or*

(c) *sailing boats, windsurfers, sailing dinghies or other craft whose principal means of propulsion is the wind but excluding craft the construction, equipment and use of which is subject to a requirement for a certificate issued pursuant to the Merchant Shipping Act 1995[c] or any regulation or order made thereunder;*

"young persons" means persons who have not attained the age of 18.

(2) Any reference in these Regulations to varying a licence includes a reference to varying a non-standard condition attached to a licence or adding or deleting such a condition from a licence.

(3) Any reference in regulation 15 to an application for a licence is a reference to an application which the licensing authority is, by virtue of regulation 4, obliged to consider.

(a) *S.I. 1996/772; as amended by S.I. 1996/1647.*
(b) *1994 c. 39.*
(c) *1995 c. 21.*

2

Regulation 3

Regulation

Persons who are required to hold a licence

(1)   Subject to paragraph (2) a person who provides facilities for adventure activities is required to hold a licence if that person -

(a)   provides such facilities in return for payment; or

(b)   is a local authority and provides the facilities to an educational establishment in respect of the pupils of such an establishment;

and where that person provides those facilities at or from more than one activity centre, and operates those activity centres at the same time throughout any period of 28 days or more, a separate licence shall be required in respect of the facilities provided at or from each such centre.

(2)   A person is not required to hold a licence in respect of facilities for adventure activities where those facilities are provided -

(a)   by a voluntary association -

(i)   to its members;

(ii)   to the members of some other voluntary association pursuant to an agreement between the associations; or

(iii)   to persons who are not its members for the purpose only of encouraging interest in its activities or attracting new members; provided that such facilities shall not be provided, in respect of any one person, on more than three days in any period of twelve months;

(b)   by an educational establishment to pupils of that establishment;

(c)   to young persons who are, during their participation in the activities in question, accompanied -

(i)   by an individual who is their parent or guardian or who has parental responsibility for them within the meaning of the Children Act 1989[a]; or

(ii)   by an individual who has parental rights within the meaning of the Law Reform (Parent and Child) (Scotland) Act 1986[b] in respect of them or, on and after the day on which section 1 of the Children (Scotland) Act 1995[c] has come into force, has parental responsibilities for them within the meaning of that section; or

(d)   under the authority of a licence held by some other person.

(a)   1989 c. 41.
(b)   1986 c. 9.
(c)   1995 c. 36.

3

Regulation 4

Regulation

4

Applications for licences

The licensing authority shall consider an application for a licence where -

(a)   *the application is made in a form and manner approved by the authority;*

(b)   *the application is accompanied by such supporting documentation as the authority reasonably requires; and*

(c)   *the required fee has been paid.*

Regulation 5

Regulation 5

Payment of fee

A fee of £620 shall be payable by the applicant to the licensing authority on each application for a licence or renewal of a licence.

Regulation 6

Regulation

6

Consideration of applications for licences

(1)   The licensing authority may grant or refuse a licence but, without prejudice to its discretion to refuse a licence on other grounds, the authority shall not grant a licence unless -

(a)   *it is satisfied that the applicant has -*

(i)   *made a suitable and sufficient assessment of the risks to the safety of the young persons and other persons who will be engaged in the adventure activities in respect of which the application is made or whose safety may be affected thereby;*

(ii)   *identified the control measures he needs to take in consequence of that assessment to ensure, so far as is reasonably practicable, the safety of those persons;*

(iii)   *made the arrangements referred to in regulation 9(1)(a) and (b);*

(iv)   *appointed competent persons to advise him on safety matters or has competence in such matters himself; and*

(b)   *the required fee has been paid.*

(2)   The licensing authority shall, before reaching a decision as to whether or not it will grant a licence, first consider a report made to the authority by a person authorised by it for that purpose pursuant to regulation 12.

(3)   The report referred to in paragraph (2) shall be made only following an inspection by the person making the report and, subject to regulation 7(2), carried out after the application for the licence has been received.

(4)   The inspection referred to in paragraph (3) shall be of any such places, equipment and documents as the person making the inspection thinks necessary for the purpose of enabling the licensing authority to satisfy itself on the matters referred to in paragraph (1).

Regulation

7

Renewal of licences

(1)   Where the licensing authority has received an application for the renewal of a licence not less than 3 months but not more than 6 months before the expiry date of that licence, then that licence shall (subject to regulation 15(2)) be regarded as continuing in force until such time as a decision is issued on that application by the authority.

(2)   In the case of an application for a renewal of a licence, the licensing authority may rely, for the purposes of regulation 6(3), upon a report based on an inspection made in respect of the licence within a period of one year before the date on which the renewal is to commence.

Regulation

8

Grant of licences

A licence granted by the licensing authority shall be in writing and shall state -

(a)   the name and address of the licence-holder;

(b)   the facilities for adventure activities which may be provided pursuant to the licence;

(c)   where the licence is issued in respect of a particular activity centre, the address of the centre concerned;

(d)   the date on which the licence will commence and the date on which the licence will expire which shall be no longer than 3 years from the date of its commencement; and

(e)   the conditions subject to which the licence has been granted.

Regulation

9

Conditions

(1)   The licensing authority shall attach the following conditions to all licences -

(a)   that the licence-holder shall maintain such arrangements as are appropriate for the review of the assessment referred to in regulation 6(1)(a)(i) and for the effective implementation, control, monitoring and review of the control measures referred to in regulation 6(1)(a)(ii);

(b)   that the licence-holder shall maintain suitable and sufficient arrangements -

(i)   for the appointment of a sufficient number of competent and adequately qualified instructors;

(ii)   for the giving of safety information to instructors and participants;

(iii)   for the provision of such equipment as is needed to ensure that the activities are carried out safely;

(iv)   for the maintenance of that equipment in an efficient state and in good repair; and

Regulation

(v) for the provision of first-aid, for the summoning of medical and rescue services in the event of an emergency, and for otherwise dealing with an emergency;

(c) that the licence-holder shall ensure that he is advised by competent persons on safety matters unless he has competence in such matters himself;

(d) that the licence-holder shall ensure that the authority is permitted to inspect at any reasonable time any place or equipment used in, or in connection with, the provision of the facilities for adventure activities to which the licence relates and any documents held by or on behalf of the licence-holder relating to such provision;

(e) that the licence-holder shall accede to any reasonable request for information from the authority relating to the provision of such facilities;

(f) that where such facilities are provided at or from an activity centre on two or more consecutive days, the licence-holder shall display at that centre a copy of the licence; and that where such facilities are not so provided the licence-holder shall have available for inspection, at any reasonable time, such a copy; and

(g) that the licence-holder shall not refer to his holding of a licence, in any advertisement or information issued by him or on his behalf, unless that reference states which adventure activities are covered by the licence and gives the telephone number of the licensing authority.

(2) The licensing authority may attach to the licence such other conditions relating to safety as it considers necessary.

9

Revocation or variation of licences

Regulation 10

Regulation

(1) Subject to the provisions of the Schedule the licensing authority may at any time revoke or vary a licence -

(a) on application being made to it by the licence-holder;

(b) if there has been a contravention of any condition attached to the licence;

(c) if any information supplied by the holder of the licence is false in any material particular; or

(d) if it considers such a revocation or variation necessary to ensure safety.

(2) The provisions of regulation 4(a) and (b) shall apply to an application for the variation of a licence as if the references in that regulation to an application for a licence were references to an application for the variation.

(3) Where a licence is revoked or varied pursuant to this regulation–

(a) the licensing authority shall give notice in writing or electronic form to the licence-holder informing him of the revocation or, as the case may be, giving details of the variation; and

10

(b)   the licence-holder shall, if so required by the licensing authority, return the licence to the authority and the authority shall, if the licence is to be varied, reissue the licence to the licence-holder in a varied form.

Complaints

(1)   The licensing authority shall consider any complaints which it receives relating to the provision of facilities for adventure activities by licence-holders and shall, if it considers it necessary, cause those complaints to be investigated.

(2)   Following the investigation of a complaint the authority shall take such action as it considers appropriate and, in particular, it may -

(a)   revoke or vary the relevant licence in accordance with regulation 10;

(b)   refer the matter to the relevant enforcing authority.

(3)   Where a complaint has been investigated by the authority the authority shall advise the complainant of the result of that investigation and of any action taken by it in consequence.

Exercise of functions by authorised persons

(1)   The licensing authority may authorise suitably experienced or qualified persons (whether or not its officers or employees) to exercise any function conferred on the authority pursuant to these Regulations.[a]

(2)   Any person authorised by the licensing authority to conduct investigations or carry out inspections shall be required to carry and produce on request a written authorisation from the authority stating the functions exercisable by that person and the period for which the authorisation will remain in force.

(a)   Substituted by SI 2007/446

The register of licences and provision of information

(1)   The licensing authority shall keep, in such form as it considers appropriate, a register of licences which shall include the name and address of each licence-holder, a description of the facilities for adventure activities which may be provided pursuant to each licence and, where the licence is issued in respect of a particular activity centre, the address of the centre concerned.

(2)   The licensing authority shall make the register available for public inspection without charge during reasonable office hours and shall allow copies to be taken on payment of such charge, if any, as it may reasonably require.

(3)   Without prejudice to paragraph (2), the licensing authority shall provide information, without charge, to any person seeking to know whether certain named persons are licence-holders but the information which the authority is obliged to provide under this paragraph shall be limited to a request in respect of no more than five such named persons.

Requirements for notifications relating to licences

The Schedule (requirements for notifications to applicants and licence-holders) shall have effect.

Appeals

(1)   An applicant for a licence may appeal to the relevant national authority against the refusal of a licence and, subject to paragraph (2), for the purposes of this regulation a failure to issue a decision on an application within three months of the date on which the application was received by the licensing authority shall be treated as a refusal.

(2)   In respect of an application for the renewal of a licence to which the provisions of regulation 7(1) apply, a failure to issue a decision within 3 months of the date of expiry of the existing licence shall be treated as a refusal.

(3)   A licence-holder may appeal to the relevant national authority against -

(a)   any non-standard condition attached to a licence;

(b)   the revocation or variation of a licence; or

(c)   the refusal to vary a licence.

(4)   Before the determination of an appeal the relevant national authority shall ask the appellant and the licensing authority whether they wish to appear and be heard on the appeal and -

(a)   if both of them express a wish not to appear and be heard, the appeal may be determined without a hearing of the parties;

(b)   if either of the parties expresses a wish to appear and be heard, the relevant national authority shall afford to both of them an opportunity of so doing.

(5)   The Health and Safety Licensing Appeals (Hearings Procedure) Rules 1974[a] or the Health and Safety Licensing Appeals (Hearings Procedure) (Scotland) Rules 1974[b] (as appropriate) shall apply to hearings under paragraph (4) as they apply to hearings in pursuance of section 44(3) of the 1974 Act.

(6)   In determining an appeal the relevant national authority may make an order -

(a)   dismissing the appeal;

(b)   allowing the appeal; or

(c)   directing the licensing authority to reconsider any matter which is the subject of the appeal.

(7)   If the relevant national authority allows the appeal it shall direct the licensing authority -

(a)   where the appeal is against refusal of a licence, to grant a licence on the conditions specified in regulation 9(1) and on such other conditions relating to safety, if any, as may be specified in the direction;

<table>
<tr><td>Regulation</td><td></td></tr>
</table>

(b) where the appeal is against any non-standard condition attached to a licence, to remove the condition or vary it in the way specified in the direction;

(c) where the appeal is against the revocation of a licence, to reinstate the licence with such variations, if any, as may be specified in the direction; or

(d) where the appeal is against the variation of a licence or against the refusal to vary a licence, to reinstate the licence in the form in which it was before the variation or to vary the licence in the way specified in the direction.

(a)   S.I. 1974/2040.
(b)   S.I. 1974/2068.

Regulation 16

Offences

(1) It is an offence for a person to do anything for which a licence is required to be held by him under these Regulations without a licence or otherwise than in accordance with such a licence.

(2) It is an offence for a person for the purposes of obtaining or holding a licence -

(a) to make a statement to the licensing authority (or someone acting on its behalf) knowing it to be false in a material particular, or

(b) recklessly to make a statement to the licensing authority (or someone acting on its behalf) which is false in a material particular.

Regulation 17

Application of enforcement provisions of health and safety legislation

Sections 18 to 25, 26, 27, 33(1)(e) to (i), (n) and (o) and (2) to (4), 34(2) to (6), 36(1), 37 to 42 and 46 of the 1974 Act shall apply for the purposes of providing for the enforcement of these Regulations and in respect of proceedings for a contravention thereof as if –

(a) references to relevant statutory provisions were references to those provisions applied by this regulation and to these Regulations; and

(b) the reference in section 33(2) to paragraph (d) of subsection (1) were omitted.

Regulation 18

Annual report

The licensing authority shall as soon as possible after 31 March in each year prepare and submit to the Health and Safety Commission and to the relevant national authority a report on the carrying out of the functions of the authority over the period of twelve months preceding that date.

Transitional Provisions

(1)   The provisions of Schedule 1 (Fees) to the Adventure Activities Licensing Regulations 1996 shall continue to apply in relation to an application for the renewal of a licence referred to in paragraph (2) provided that -

(a)   any fee payable is made before the date of expiry of that licence; and

(b)   the application for renewal is received by the licensing authority before the date of the coming into force of these Regulations.

(2)   Paragraph (1) applies to a licence in respect of which the date of expiry falls on or after the date of the coming into force of these Regulations but on or before the date three months after the date of the coming into force of these Regulations.

Revocation

(1)   The 1996 Regulations are, subject to paragraph (2), hereby revoked.

(2)   The 1996 Regulations shall, until the date three months after the date of the coming into force of these Regulations, continue in force so far as is necessary to give effect to the provisions of regulation 19 of these Regulations.

Regulation

19

Regulation

20

Schedule

Schedule

Requirements for notifications to applicants and licence-holders

Regulation 14

1.   In this Schedule "relevant action" means a refusal to grant or vary a licence, the imposition of any non-standard condition on the grant of a licence or the revocation of a licence.

2.   (1)   Where the licensing authority expresses to any person any opinion as to what remedial action should be taken by that person, if that person so requests, the authority -

(a)   shall as soon as practicable give to him a notice in writing or electronic form which satisfies the requirements of sub-paragraph (2) below; and

(b)   shall not take any relevant action against him until after the end of 28 days beginning with the giving of the notice.

(2)   A notice satisfies the requirement of this sub-paragraph if it -

(a)   states the nature of the remedial action which in the opinion of the authority should be taken, and explains why and within what period;

(b)   in the case where the authority is of the opinion that a condition of a licence is not being complied with, explains what constitutes the failure to comply with that condition; and

(c)   states the nature of the relevant action which could be taken and states the effect of paragraph 3 below and of regulation 15 (appeals).

3.   Before the licensing authority takes any relevant action against any person, the authority -

(a)   shall give to that person notice in writing or electronic form -

(i)   that it is considering taking the action and the reasons why; and

(ii)   that the person may, within a period specified in the notice, make in writing or electronic form representations to the authority or, if the person so requests, make oral representations to the authority; and

(iii) shall consider any representations which are duly made and not withdrawn.

4.   Where the licensing authority has taken relevant action against any person the authority shall, as soon as practicable, give to that person a notice in writing or in electronic form explaining the effect of regulation 15 (appeals).

Explanatory note
(This note is not part of the Regulations)

These Regulations revoke and re-enact with modifications the Adventure Activities Licensing Regulations 1996. The Regulations provide for the licensing of persons

Schedule

in respect of the provision of facilities for adventure activities (as defined). The Regulations apply to England, Scotland and Wales.

In addition to minor and drafting amendments, the Regulations make the following changes of substance.

The Regulations provide for the payment of a single fee on application for a licence or a renewal of a licence (regulation 5). The specified fee is £620. This replaces the former requirement for a basic fee of £200 on application and an additional inspection fee calculated on the basis of £200 plus a further sum of £30 per hour based on the number of hours of inspection, subject to a maximum inspection fee of £1200. In respect of an application for a variation of a licence, the former charge of £100 is now waived.

The Regulations -

(a)   provide for an existing licence, in specified circumstances, to continue in force for a maximum period of three months (regulation 7(1) and 15(2));

(b)   provide that, in granting a licence on application for renewal, the licensing authority may rely on an inspection carried out within 12 months prior to the date of expiry (regulation 7(2));

(c)   enable the relevant national authority (as defined) to determine an appeal by referring any matter back to the licensing authority (regulation 15(6));

(d)   require the licensing authority to send an annual report to the relevant national authority in addition to the Health and Safety Commission (regulation 18).

The Regulations provide for transitional provisions in relation to the payment of fees (regulation 19).

A copy of the regulatory impact assessment prepared in respect of these Regulations can be obtained from the Department for Education and Skills, Pupil Safety & School Security Team, 2B1, Sanctuary Buildings, Great Smith Street, London SW1P 3BT. A copy has been placed in the library of each House of Parliament.

Glossary

A number of terms and expressions used in this guidance are defined by regulation 2 the Adventure Activity Licensing Regulations 2004 (see Appendix 3). Such terms and expressions are used with the same meaning in this document.

Other terms used in this guidance have the following meanings:

activity any discrete part of a package or programme offered by a provider that comes within the meaning of facilities for adventure activities.

group leader an instructor who is at any time supervising one or more participants and or assistants undertaking adventure activities.

hazard anything that can cause harm.

hazard level the different environmental, seasonal or difficulty levels at which an activity may be done, as shown in the competence matrices in Appendix 2.

instructor a generic term for the instructor/leader and assistant, if present.

participants the people engaging in adventure activities, including those over 18 accompanying under 18s.

provider a person or organisation who delivers adventure activities and who is required to hold a licence under the Regulations, whether a licence-holder or an applicant for a licence.

requirements related to safety the safety matters on which the licensing authority must be satisfied before it grants a licence (regulations 6(1) and 9(1)(a) and (b)).

risk the chance, great or small, that someone will be harmed by a hazard.

staff all persons, whether contractually engaged or not, who are under the control or instruction of a person providing a licensable adventure activity.

special educational needs learning difficulties, physical limitations or behavioural problems.

Further reading

Adventure Activities Licensing Regulations 2004 SI 2004/1309 The Stationery Office 2004 ISBN 978 0 11 049305 3

Adventure Activities Licensing (Amendment) Regulations 2007 SI 2007/446 The Stationery Office 2007 ISBN 978 0 11 075826 8

Management of health and safety at work. Management of Health and Safety at Work Regulations 1999. Approved Code of Practice and guidance L21 (Second edition) HSE Books 2000 ISBN 978 0 7176 2488 1

Personal protective equipment at work (Second edition). Personal Protective Equipment at Work Regulations 1992 (as amended). Guidance on Regulations L25 (Second edition) HSE Books 2005 ISBN 978 0 7176 6139 8

Adventure activities centres: Five steps to risk assessment Guidance HSE Books 1999 ISBN 978 0 7176 2463 8

Safe use of work equipment. Provision and Use of Work Equipment Regulations 1998. Approved Code of Practice and guidance L22 (Second edition) HSE Books 1998 ISBN 978 0 7176 1626 8

Five steps to risk assessment Leaflet INDG163(rev2) HSE Books 2006 (single copy free or priced packs of 10 ISBN 978 0 7176 6189 3) Web version: www.hse.gov.uk/pubns/indg163.pdf

Essentials of health and safety at work HSE Books 2006 ISBN 978 0 7176 6179 4

A guide to the Reporting of Injuries, Diseases and Dangerous Occurrences Regulations 1995 L73 (Second edition) HSE Books 1999 ISBN 978 0 7176 2431 7

RIDDOR explained: Reporting of Injuries, Diseases and Dangerous Occurrences Regulations Leaflet HSE31(rev1) HSE Books 1999 (single copy free or priced packs of 10 ISBN 978 0 7176 2441 6)

First aid at work. The Health and Safety (First Aid) Regulations 1981. Approved Code of Practice and guidance L74 HSE Books 1997 ISBN 978 0 7176 1050 1

Successful health and safety management HSG65 (Second edition) HSE Books 1997 ISBN 978 0 7176 1276 5

Useful web addresses

Guidance on various topics related to licensing has been compiled by the licensing service and is available on their website: www.aals.org.uk

Further information

HSE priced and free publications are available by mail order from HSE Books, PO Box 1999, Sudbury, Suffolk CO10 2WA Tel: 01787 881165 Fax: 01787 313995 Website: www.hsebooks.co.uk (HSE priced publications are also available from bookshops and free leaflets can be downloaded from HSE's website: www.hse.gov.uk.)

For information about health and safety ring HSE's Infoline Tel: 0845 345 0055 Fax: 0845 408 9566 Textphone: 0845 408 9577 e-mail: hse.infoline@natbrit.com or write to HSE Information Services, Caerphilly Business Park, Caerphilly CF83 3GG.

The Stationery Office publications are available from The Stationery Office, PO Box 29, Norwich NR3 1GN Tel: 0870 600 5522 Fax: 0870 600 5533 e-mail: customer.services@tso.co.uk Website: www.tso.co.uk (They are also available from bookshops.) Statutory Instruments can be viewed free of charge at www.opsi.gov.uk.

Printed and published by the Health and Safety Executive   C25   08/07